I. INTRODUCTION

Mergers in the United States are regulated by Section 7 of the Clayton Act, which proscribes transactions that may substantially lessen competition or create a monopoly. The courts have some latitude to interpret the law, and recent decisions have varied from *Consolidated Gold Fields v. Anglo American*, in which a merger was enjoined because it marginally increased concentration in an oligopolistic industry, to *U. S. vs. Syufy Enterprises* in which a merger to near monopoly was considered legal due to the lack of entry barriers. Although all of these decisions are subject to review by the Supreme Court, the Court has not reviewed the merits of a merger case in the 1980s. This paper applies statistical techniques to investigate the underpinnings of horizontal merger decisions over the last ten years.

Although evolving merger standards are discussed almost annually in the <u>Antitrust Law Journal</u> of the American Bar Association and an occasional law journal article has highlighted specific trends, economists have given little attention to reviewing merger decisions.[1] In an appendix to their study of settlements, Langenfeld and Rogowsky (1984) presented a probit model of the 40 federal merger cases litigated between 1968 and 1981. They found that the market share of the acquiring firm and the Federal Trade Commission (FTC) as a plaintiff increased the probability of a merger injunction, while a time trend variable

---

[1] Reprints of articles on mergers from the <u>Antitrust Law Journal</u> and various law journals are presented in volume 21-2 of the <u>Journal of Reprints for Antitrust Law and Economics</u> (Coate (1992-A).

suggested that the government was less likely to win cases filed in the late 1970s. More recently, in the final section of a study of the effect of the government's Merger Guidelines on court decisions, Coate (1992-B) found that the Herfindahl index, efficiencies and other structural characteristics related to anticompetitive effects influenced the likelihood of the government obtaining a merger injunction in industries exhibiting barriers to entry. Assuming no other structural conditions were identified, a Herfindahl of 2400 was shown to generate an 88 percent probability of a merger injunction. However, the presence of efficiencies and buyer power would combine to reduce the chance of an injunction to 59 percent.

The goal of this paper is to analyze empirically the decision-making process of the federal courts. The next two sections present a discussion of the case law and an overview of the available data. The cases generally focus on the likely competitive effect of a merger, with evidence on market shares, barriers to entry, efficiencies and structural conditions affecting the outcome of the court decision. The data suggest that the Department of Justice (DOJ) is less likely to prevail on the merits than either the FTC or private plaintiffs, while no clear patterns emerge for the inferred political affiliation of the deciding panel of judges or the evolution of the law over time. Section IV presents econometric models of both the court's decision on the merits and the underlying findings on barriers to entry and conditions compatible with either pro- or anti-competitive effects.

Overall, merger decisions appear to be driven by the economic merits of the cases, while the specific barrier or competitive effect findings seem to depend on the type of case and identification of the plaintiff. The conclusion highlights the implications of the models, suggesting that plaintiffs (other than the DOJ) are more likely to prevail in preliminary injunction cases than full trials on the merits.

II. AN OVERVIEW OF MERGER LAW

Merger enforcement is generally based on the *Philadelphia National Bank* decision, in which the Supreme Court ruled high concentration established a rebuttable presumption of illegality (Bork(1978). The level of evidence sufficient to rebut the presumption appears to have evolved over the years. While one could read some early Supreme Court decisions (*Von's Grocery* and *Brown Shoe*) as establishing almost a *per-se* rule against mergers in concentrated industries, the *General Dynamics* decision highlighted the importance of competitive factors other than market share. The Court ruled that full consideration of a market's "structure, history and probable future" was necessary to measure the competitive impact of a transaction. While the identity of the various factors was initially unclear, a consensus on the key factors developed in the 1980s. We highlight entry, efficiencies, buyer power, and general competitive factors in the discussion below.

Entry was elevated to a crucial position in merger analysis by the 1984 *Waste Management* decision. In reversing a district court's divestiture order, the Second Circuit generalized the concept of potential competition to require consideration of the ease of entry in a merger case.[2] A number of other cases (*Calmar, Echlin, Occidental Petroleum* and *Red Foods*) throughout the 1980s built on the *Waste Management* decision, culminating in the *Syufy* case in which the Ninth Circuit Court of Appeals upheld a decision dismissing a challenge of a merger to near monopoly on the grounds of easy entry. The only case that did not require a showing of barriers was *R. C. Bigelow v. Unilever* (at p. 111). In this merger, the appeals court ruled an 84 percent post-merger market share was sufficient to create a genuine issue for trial, even though the district court opinion appeared to imply that barriers to entry did not exist.

The DOJ attempted to raise the burden associated with an entry defense in the *Baker Hughes* (at p. 987) case. However, Judge, now Supreme Court Justice, Clarence Thomas ruled that the DOJ's proposed "quick and effective" standard would have imposed an undue burden of proving entry will occur on the defendants. As an alternative, Judge Thomas stated that the evaluation of entry conditions should be based on the totality of the evidence.

Overall, it appears that the case law basically requires a showing of entry barriers, if hypothetical anticompetitive behavior is going to be inferred from a Herfindahl statistic. Barriers are

---

[2] For a more detailed discussion of the evolution of entry analysis, see Coate and Langenfeld (1993).

usually identified as factors that delay entry for a significant period of time, although conditions that require the entrants to compete at higher cost levels are sometimes noted. Assuming barriers to entry do not exist, mergers are very unlikely to be blocked.

Efficiencies also play a role in merger analysis, although more as a factor that should be considered in interpreting the Herfindahl statistic. Numerous courts have cited efficiencies as a factor that should be considered in merger analysis (Coate (1992-B)). For example, in *Owens Illinois* (at p. 53), the court found that Owens Illinois' claim that it could improve the performance of its target, Brockway, more persuasive than the government's contentions that the efficiencies were speculative. In both *PPG* and *Elders Grain*, the district courts discussed efficiencies, but enjoined the transactions because the mergers were likely to lessen competition. Other decisions have recognized the theoretical importance of efficiencies, but failed to find efficiencies in the facts of the case at hand (see for example, *American Medical International* (at pp. 215-220)). In the most recent case, the Eleventh Circuit ruled in *University Health* (at p. 1222) that (merger-specific) efficiencies can rebut the government's case, but University Hospital did not come forward with sufficient evidence to show that efficiencies existed. No court decision has attempted to undertake a short run balancing of the welfare triangle and cost savings (as described in Williamson (1968)).

Buyer power has also been cited as a factor that makes

anticompetitive pricing less likely. Two different strands of the analysis appear to exist (Steptoe(1993)). First, buyer power affects competition through its ability to facilitate entry. In *Country Lake Foods* (at 64,117), the court found that the larger customers of milk would seek out new sources of supply in response to higher prices after the merger. This analytical insight is not independent of the entry discussion (see above), and thus buyer power would be a factor to consider in evaluating ease of entry and not competitive effects.

The other approach to buyer power involves a theoretical link to market performance, with large buyers having some direct influence on competition. The most obvious theory is bilateral monopoly in which a large buyer group negotiates with the large sellers and hopefully ends up with a competitive market.[3] The facts in *Country Lake Foods* would appear to fit this model, with three firms purchasing 90 percent of the milk output. It is also possible to factor buyer power into a model of competitive effect. By shifting purchases among the cartel members, a large buyer could disrupt the mutual trust necessary to maintain prices above the competitive level. Alternatively, a large buyer could aggregate its requirements into a single purchase to present the collusive firms with an attractive opportunity to cheat on their agreement. If the tacit collusion disintegrates, the market would return to the competitive level. Judge Posner applied this analysis of buyer

---

[3] Suppliers may be able to negotiate with the customers to maintain the monopoly price and share the anticompetitive profits. See Blair et al. (1989).

power in *Elders Grain*, but found it insufficient to ensure competitive performance. On the other hand, the court in *Archer Daniels Midland* (at 1418) noted a number of these tactics could be employed by large buyers of high fructose corn syrup. Thus, collusion was unlikely to succeed at maintaining higher prices (see also, *Owens Illinois*, *Occidental Petroleum*, and *Donnelley*[4]). Another theory suggests that sophisticated buyers can maintain competitive prices by threatening the collusive firms with a loss of business in other markets. A multiproduct firm could be unwilling to risk a broad business relationship with a customer for collusive profits in one narrow market. This approach could have been applied in *Baker Hughes*, because the district court found that customers have need for various types of equipment manufactured by the merging parties.

Overall, the buyer power concept includes two different analytical techniques. One analysis directly addresses the entry issue and is likely to play an important role deciding the ease of entry issue (see, Kleit and Coate (1993)). The other approach notes buyer power represents one point that must be integrated into a competitive effects evaluation of the merger.

Numerous other structural factors play a role in the

---

[4] In *Occidental Petroleum* (at 62,518), the court found customers played suppliers off against each other and this pressure would tend to keep prices at the competitive level. A similar story existed in *Owens Illinois* (at 48), with the buyers able to use large orders to bargain for competitive prices. Moreover, in *Donnelley* (at 64,855), the district court found the large customers could use their size and economic power to preserve competition.

evaluation of the merger's competitive effect. It is well known that characteristics such as homogeneous products, demand inelasticity, static technology and similar cost structures make collusion relatively more likely. Various cases, such as *Bass Brothers* and *HCA*, present these types of facts as enhancing the concerns associated with the Herfindahl. On the other hand, factors like heterogenous products, low capacity utilization and minimal market information make collusion more difficult. Other cases, like *Echlin* and *Archer Daniels Midland*, involve a number of factors that make collusion less likely. Hence these factors lower the concerns associated with the Herfindahl index. Finally, cases like *Weyerhaeuser* (at 288), *Owens Illinois* (at 50), and *Carilion Health System* (at 849) find the elasticity of fringe supply is sufficiently elastic to defeat an anticompetitive price increase.

Court cases include references to numerous structural variables that either enhance or militate against competitive concerns. In fact, any factor that can be linked to the three oligopolistic problems of obtaining a tacit agreement, detecting deviations from the tacit agreement and punishing deviations from the tacit agreement can be integrated into the legal/economic analysis. The court decisions do not give any obvious way of weighing the various economic factors in the legal decision.

In conclusion, an empirical investigation of merger decisions would expect to find liability positively related to both concentration and factors associated with the likelihood of an anticompetitive effect. On the other hand, lack of barriers, efficiencies, buyer power and factors incompatible with collusion would likely be linked with the lack of liability. In the next section, we take an initial look at the available economic and institutional data associated with merger cases.

III. AN OVERVIEW OF THE DATA

In the little more than ten years since the 1982 revision of the Merger Guidelines, almost 50 merger cases have been decided on the merits. In the federal courts, these cases are almost equally divided among the DOJ (15 cases, with five preliminary injunctions), the FTC (14 cases, all preliminary injunctions), and private parties or state governments (13 cases, all but two preliminary injunctions).[5] Moreover, the FTC has completed a number of administrative trials which would add another six decisions to the analysis.[6] A review of these decisions would

---

[5] Two private cases involved affirmative decisions on standing. Before the court could issue a decision on the injunction, the transactions collapsed. Given the cases would not have obtained standing without evidence on antitrust injury (see, *Monfort*), preliminary injunctions were very likely to issue and the cases are counted as enjoined mergers.

[6] The data set includes 42 federal court decisions with findings on the merits of the antitrust complaint issued between 1982 and 1992. Numerous other cases were filed, but ended either in settlements or were rejected by the courts due to lack of standing. The data set also includes the six FTC decisions noted in Coate (1992-B). Administrative Law Judge decisions in Coke-Southwest, Textron-Avdel, Coke-Dr. Pepper, Occidental-Tennaco and Ukiah Hospital were on appeal to the Commission in late 1992 and a Commission divestiture order in Olin/FMC was on appeal to the Ninth Circuit in December 1992. All of these incomplete decisions are excluded from the analysis. The FTC's dismissal of the complaint in Owens Illinois was issued in 1992, but was not included in the study, because the district court's rejection of a preliminary injunction is part of the data set.

show that the plaintiff prevailed in blocking the merger in 25 of the 48 cases, for a success rate of a little more than 50 percent. Thus, Justice Stewart's *Von's Grocery* comment that "the Government always wins" no longer appears to be true.

Preliminary injunctions differ from full trials on the merits in two respects. First, the plaintiff is only required to show a likelihood of success on the merits, instead of bearing a burden of proof on the likely competitive effects. Given court decisions involve an inference of the likely competitive effect of a merger from legal findings on markets, concentration, barriers, competitive conditions and efficiencies, a difference in standards would have to be addressed at the level of the court findings. For example, courts could require less evidence for an affirmative finding of barriers to entry in a preliminary injunction, which would implicitly increase the likelihood of a merger injunction. Thus, it should be possible to search for general decision rules that are used to balance various factual findings, with a difference in standards observed for the actual findings. Second, a preliminary injunction matter requires some balancing of the equities, with the specific rule depending on type of plaintiff. However, this requirement only appears to address the magnitude of the relief, with court decisions showing evidence of a likely anticompetitive effect creating a strong equity in favor of an injunction (see *PPG Industries*). At best, the parties could hope for a hold separate order, until the full trial on the merits (see *Weyerhaeuser*). Thus, the equities would only appear to affect the form of the relief, not the underlying standards of analysis.

Table 1 presents an overview of the outcomes of all 48 cases classified by type of plaintiff. The columns define the winning percentages for the DOJ, the FTC (with the percentage for the FTC's federal court preliminary injunctions in parenthesis), the private or state plaintiffs and the entire sample.[7] One can see that the DOJ has had the most problems winning cases, with a success rate of 27 percent. In comparison, both the FTC and private parties appear to be statistically more likely to win, with percentages over 60 percent, while the overall sample mean was 52 percent. Similar results are observed if the data are split into preliminary injunction cases and full trials on the merits. For preliminary injunctions, the DOJ wins 20 percent of their cases, while the FTC and private parties win a significantly higher 70 percent of the time. This result tends to disappear for the full trials on the merits with the DOJ's success rate rising to 30 percent and the FTC's winning percentage falling to 50 percent. The two private cases in this category ended with a judgement for the defendants.

---

[7] It is impossible to statistically confirm one circuit is better than another due to the limited number of cases. However, circuit-shopping will no doubt continue since a number of circuits have their key appeals court decisions (9th - Syufy, DC - Baker Hughes and 2nd - Consolidated Gold), while other circuits have well known Appeals Court judges (7th - Judges Posner and Easterbrook; DC - Judge Douglas Ginsburg). Others may look at the record with some circuits appearing to favor plaintiffs (7th - four wins, no defeats; 6th - four wins, one defeat and 9th - six wins, three defeat) and other Circuits favoring defendants (3rd - two wins, four defeats; 4th - zero wins, two defeats; and 8th - zero wins, two defeats). Finally, it would appear some circuits could be chosen, because they have no recent track record on the merits (1st, 10th - no cases).

Two additional rows show the winning percentages for courts controlled by judges or Commissioners appointed by either Republican or Democratic presidents.[8] The plaintiff's winning percentage is usually higher for courts appointed by Republicans, although the differences are not statistically significant. Thus, the identification of the political party that appointed the court does not appear to affect the difference in winning percentage. The next two rows focus on the winning percentages over time. The differences in winning percentages for 1982 to 1986 and for 1987 to 1992 are all small and insignificant, hence we have no evidence to support the hypothesis that merger standards changed over the 1980s.

The final two rows show how successful the plaintiffs are at meeting their burden to show a concentrated market subject to an anticompetitive effect (the rebuttable presumption in *Philadelphia National Bank*) and then of prevailing on the merits. Overall, a review of the data shows plaintiffs manage to establish a concentrated market adversely affected by the merger in 75 percent of their cases, with the FTC doing better (at 90 percent) and the DOJ and private parties having slightly lower averages.[9] This implies that the DOJ's lower success rate (at least relative to private parties) does not appear to be related to market

---

[8] A court is considered Republican if either the district judge or over 50 percent of the voting Commissioners or reviewing Court of Appeals panel were appointed by Republican Presidents.

[9] A market is considered concentrated if the Herfindahl exceeds 1000 and the change in the Herfindahl exceeds 100 points.

definition. The final row shows the litigation success rates for those cases in which the presumption is met. This time the private parties have a perfect record, while the FTC obtained injunctions in 72 percent of their cases. The DOJ had a success rate of 40 percent, which is statistically lower than the success rate of private parties.

Any analysis of winning percentages in merger cases implicitly assumes that the underlying economic merits of the cases are the same. Since merger analyses generally follow the standard format of first reaching a decision on relevant market, then measuring the level of concentration, next addressing ease of entry, and finally measuring the other factors that influence the competitive effect of the merger, it is relatively easy to review the public court decisions and tabulate the judge's findings. Information on the Herfindahl statistic, the change in the Herfindahl, the presence of barriers to entry, the economic conditions conducive to and incompatible with noncompetitive behavior (including buyer power) and the existence of efficiencies are all collected from the court opinions. The study used the analyses included in the highest court decision for each merger case, but looked back to lower court decisions for facts that were omitted from an Appeals Court decision. In some cases, Herfindahl and change in Herfindahl statistics were estimated from the market share data in the court decisions (see Coate(1992-B)). A binary variable was used to proxy barriers to entry, taking on the value one if entry was considered impeded by the court and zero otherwise. Information from the court decision on structural conditions linked to either continued competitive performance or post-merger anticompetitive effects was recorded and summarized in two indices, one reporting the number of competitive factors noted in the decision supportive of competitive post-merger behavior and the other noting the number of factors linked to potential anticompetitive conduct. The data on buyer power were also recorded separately, with a dummy variable taking on a value of one if the court found any form of power buyer.[10] Finally, an efficiency variable was tabulated with a value of one representing cases in which the court found the merger offered some efficiencies and a value of zero for the cases in which court findings did not support an efficiency defense.

Data on the merits of the various cases are presented in Table 2 for a 40 observation data set focusing on the cases where detailed economic findings were made.[11] As the table notes, the sample includes 12 of the 15 DOJ cases, 19 of the 20 FTC cases and 9 of the 13 private or state cases. The second row presents the adjusted winning percentages ranging from 33 percent for the DOJ to a significantly higher 68 percent for the FTC and almost 90 percent for the private cases. These averages are higher than the overall

---

[10] In general, the court decisions suggest that buyer power can both facilitate entry and disrupt collusive pricing.

[11] This sample includes 36 cases in which the plaintiff established a presumption of an anticompetitive effect and four cases in which court made alternative findings for the plaintiff's market. In these four cases, the court found for the defendant on market definition and dismissed the case. However, the decisions also included alternative findings for the plaintiff's market which are used in this study.

sample, because the eight merger cases deleted due to the lack of information were all dismissed by the courts. The average Herfindahl index approaches 4000 for both the private and DOJ cases and was just slightly lower for the FTC. Thus, the average case involves a Herfindahl over twice the critical DOJ Guidelines level of 1800. The change in Herfindahl statistic displayed a similar pattern, with the average change above 1000 for each type of plaintiff. Neither the differences in the Herfindahl or in the change in Herfindahl are statistically significant for the three types of plaintiff. Thus, one can only conclude that the average market concentration associated with each type of plaintiff is similar.

The table also highlights the consideration given to barriers, efficiencies and buyer power. The DOJ's lower success rate appears to stem from a failure to show barriers to entry. Both the private parties and the FTC succeeded in showing barriers in roughly 80 percent of their cases, while the DOJ had approximately half the success rate at 42 percent. This difference is marginally significant (t-statistic 1.64) for the private cases and strongly significant for the FTC cases (t-statistic 2.38). Government cases in federal court, brought by either the DOJ or FTC, were more likely to involve affirmative findings of efficiencies than cases brought by private parties, with the efficiency differences generating t-statistics of around 1.5 (t-statistic 1.57 for the DOJ, 1.46 for the FTC, and 1.85 for the combined sample). A similar pattern is found for buyer power, although the result is not statistically significant. Thus, the DOJ's lower winning percentage may be related to a difficulty establishing barriers to entry in cases it chose to bring, while private plaintiff's high winning percentage may be linked to the observation that defendants have had trouble showing efficiencies.

The next three variables focus more broadly on the other structural characteristics. The eighth row presents the mean number of conditions conducive to an anticompetitive effect implicitly listed in a court decision. On average, the DOJ appeared to obtain a lower number of conditions than either the FTC or private parties, with the FTC advantage being statistically significant (t-statistic 2.17). The next row presents the average number of conditions compatible with competition. The DOJ was also more likely to have conditions (such as buyer power) cited as incompatible with an anticompetitive effect, although the difference is only significant for private parties (t-statistic 1.88). The final row calculates the net conditions favorable to a merger injunction by subtracting both the procompetitive conditions and the efficiency findings from the number of conditions compatible with collusion. This figure defines an index with which to measure the likely competitive impact of the transaction. Not surprisingly, the DOJ has a significantly lower index than either the FTC (t-statistic 1.84) or private parties (t-statistic 2.32).

It is also possible to use the economic merits data to determine if the likelihood of prevailing in court depends on the inferred political affiliation of the judge(s) or the time at which

16

the final decision was rendered. Under the Priest and Klein (1984) selection model of litigation, the merits of the cases that are ultimately litigated would change if the decision rule was altered. Thus, if over time, the courts shift to a weaker liability standard or if the case is assigned to a more lenient judge or panel, stronger cases would be brought to trial, but the winning probability would remain relatively constant.[12] Thus, the Priest and Klein model would suggest that different standards are being employed if the merits variables differed significantly with respect to politics or time. Means and variances for the Herfindahl, Barrier, Conditions Anticompetitive, Conditions Procompetitive and Efficiency variables were calculated, both for the 25 Republican court cases and 15 Democratic court cases and for the 18 cases before January 1, 1987 and the 22 cases after January 1, 1987. No significant differences in any of the merits' variables were identified, suggesting that, for both politics and time, the legal decision structure does not depend on the

---

[12] The Priest and Klein model allows for small changes in winning percentages in response to regime shifts, but highlights a general evolution to a fixed winning percentage which approximates 50 percent if the stakes of both parties are identical. If lower court decisions were constrained by the Supreme Court's implicit understanding of merger law, the political variables would not affect the outcome. However, the time index would proxy both political changes in the Supreme Court (becoming more Republican over the entire time period) and any evolution of the merger standard. If the assumptions (primarily the ability of both parties to predict the outcome of the case with random error) for the Priest and Klein selection hypothesis are not applicable to merger cases, evidence that the merits of the cases are similar for the two subsamples of cases, coupled with the similarities in the winning percentage would suggest that merger standards do not depend on politics or time (within the 1982-1992 period).

appointing party or the time during the Reagan/Bush era.

Although the initial review of the data highlights some results such as the DOJ's lower likelihood of establishing barriers to entry and the lack of a relationship between either politics and time and the outcome of the merger case, it is possible that other observations are masked by the aggregation of the data.[13] Thus, in the next section, we construct econometric models of merger enforcement to determine the simultaneous impact of the variables.

IV. ECONOMETRIC ANALYSIS OF COURT DECISIONS

This section presents statistical analyses of various decisions made in merger cases. In general, courts make decisions to produce two distinct types of products, rule makings and dispute resolutions (Cooter and Rubinfeld (1989 at 1072)). Both types of decisions are necessary in merger cases. Courts define implicit rules with which to balance the evidence to determine whether a

---

[13] The case reviews also shed some insight on the average number of Guideline citations in merger analysis. In our tabulation, the Merger Guidelines are cited 27 times for the Herfindahl discussion, 14 times for the barrier to entry analysis and 16 times for the competitive effects analysis. DOJ cases average 1.33 citations and the FTC cases average 1.74; the average government case exhibits 1.58 characteristics. This figure is significantly higher (t-statistic 2.32) than the average of .89 citations in the private cases. Citations to the guidelines tend to be correlated with defeat for the plaintiffs. If the guidelines are not cited, the plaintiffs prevail in 78 percent of the nine cases. However, if guidelines are cited once, the rate falls to 71 percent (14 cases). Two separate citations (eight cases) imply a slightly lower 63 percent success and if the Guidelines are cited for Herfindahls, entry and competitive analysis (nine cases), the plaintiff retains only a 44 percent chance of winning. Thus, the Guidelines appear more useful in explaining why a merger is not likely to be anticompetitive.

merger is likely to substantially lessen competition. While the rule is not explicitly written into the opinion, a statistical model may be able to identify the implicit decision methodology. In this paper, the outcome of the merger case is analyzed as a function of the Herfindahl, the existence of barriers to entry and the index for competitive conditions.

Courts must also settle a number of disputes between the parties with respect to key variables such as market definition, barriers to entry, competitive effects and efficiencies. While market definition and efficiencies are difficult to quantify, models can be constructed to evaluate how the courts resolve disputes between the parties on barriers to entry and competitive conditions. These models explore the impact of various exogenous factors, such as the identity of the plaintiff, time, and the type of litigation. By analyzing the two types of legal decisions, it is possible to distinguish factors that have a direct effect on the merger decision, from those that only indirectly affect the process through an impact on barriers to entry or competitive effects. One could argue that the explanatory variables are endogenous, with the courts making dispute resolution findings on Herfindahls, barriers, competitive conditions, and efficiencies to generate their desired outcome. However, all court decisions are subject to further judicial review, so inappropriate dispute resolutions are likely to be reversed.[14]

---

[14] In the overall sample, 15 cases were appealed and four were reversed on appeal. One case was decided after an earlier reversal on a market definition dispute.

Analysis of the Outcome of Merger Challenges

The basic model assumes that a court's decision is driven by the underlying economic factors recognized in the case. The value one is assigned to all cases that ended with merger injunctions and the value zero to all dismissed cases. This outcome variable is then explained by a probit model consisting of the level of the post-merger Herfindahl, the presence of barriers to entry and the net number of economic conditions compatible with an anticompetitive effect. This specification expands the Coate(1992-B) model to include barriers to entry.

The level of the Herfindahl statistic is expected to affect the merger decision, with higher Herfindahls more likely to be associated with merger injunctions. As market shares rise, firms may be more likely to coordinate their activity, so mergers could have an anticompetitive effect on the market. Moreover, as the Herfindahl approaches 10,000, a dominant firm may obtain monopoly power and be able to unilaterally set price. Thus, one would expect the Herfindahl index to have a significant positive effect on the likelihood of a merger crder. The binary entry barrier variable is also expected to affect the likelihood of a successful merger injunction. If the court decision concludes entry barriers are high, entrants are unable to quickly defeat a price increase, so mergers are more likely to be anticompetitive. Thus, a positive coefficient is expected for the barrier variable. The final economic variable utilizes the net number of conditions compatible with an anticompetitive effect (labeled Netcon). As noted above, the index is computed for each merger decision by subtracting the number of factors suggestive of continued competition or efficiencies from the number of conditions conducive to anticompetitive effects. In effect, this approach attempts to quantify the *Philadelphia National Bank* and *General Dynamics* requirement that various factors other than concentration enter the analysis. While one could argue whether efficiencies should be included as a separate variable, data limitations preclude this approach. As the number of conditions compatible with a noncompetitive outcome increase, one would expect the court to be more likely to enjoin the merger. Thus, a positive sign is expected for the variable. The probit parameter estimates are presented below [15]

$$WIN = -12.85 + .001656 \ HHI + 10.02 \ BARRIERS + .6728 \ Netcon$$
$$\quad (-1.59) \quad (1.62) \quad\quad (1.64) \quad\quad (2.06)$$

$$Pseudo\text{-}R^2 = .8070 \quad Chi\text{-}Square = 42.71.$$

Herfindahls, barriers and competitive conditions are all positively related to the likelihood of a merger order, although the significance level on the Herfindahl and barrier variables is marginal.[16] However, the overall model clearly passes the Chi-

---

[15] The dependent variable only takes on values of one and zero, therefore a probit technique is appropriate. Fitted values can be translated into predicted probabilities with the aid of a standard normal table.

[16] The statistical significance of the coefficients improves noticeably if the Herfindahl index is replaced by a variable that
(continued...)

square test and explains roughly 80 percent of the variance in the dependent variable. Moreover, the model generates a predicted probability of over 50 percent for 24 of the 25 cases in which the merger was enjoined and a predicted probability of success of under 50 percent for 13 of the 15 cases in which a merger injunction was denied. All told, the model successfully predicts roughly 90 percent of the court decisions.

Evaluating the model for the mean data points generates a probability of 71 percent that an injunction will be issued. This probability is 99 percent for the mean data associated with FTC or private cases, but is less than 1 percent for the average data associated with a DOJ case. Thus, the DOJ's lower likelihood of success on the merits appears clearly linked to the underlying economic structure of their markets. A similar result is found for the difference between preliminary injunction cases and full trials on the merits. The model suggests that a plaintiff has a 95 percent chance of winning a preliminary injunction matter, but only 10 percent chance of winning a full trial on the merits given the different averages for Herfindahls, barriers and conditions.

---

[16](...continued)
truncates the Herfindahl effect for relatively low concentration levels (see, Coate (1992) for a similar equation). The adjusted Herfindahl index would assume low Herfindahl cases have no effect on the outcome, so the index should be set to zero. A search for the critical Herfindahl level shows the log likelihood function is maximized at a Herfindahl cutoff of 2000, although data limitations preclude the study of lower Herfindahl numbers. The estimated equation is given below (with t-statistics in parentheses). Win = -6.461 (-1.92) + .0008376 (1.94) Adjusted HHI + 5.781 (1.99) BARRIERS + .5958 (2.46) Netcon. (Pseudo-R^2 = .7929, Chi-Square = 41.96). In general, this model generates similar implications as the standard model given in the text.

It is also possible to evaluate various scenarios with the basic model. For example, the model suggests that the plaintiff has little chance of success if barriers to entry are not present. Even assuming a post-merger Herfindahl of 7000, it would be necessary to have two findings compatible with an anticompetitive effect (and none compatible with competition) before the probability of a merger injunction would exceed 50 percent. Thus, the model seems to suggest that barriers are almost a necessary condition for an anticompetitive effect.

If barriers to entry are present, a complaint is not guaranteed. Assuming the Herfindahl is 2400 and the net condition variable (Netcon) is zero, the merger would have a 87 percent chance of being enjoined in the basic model. Now assuming the court found two factors suggesting continued competition (the Netcon variable would be -2), the likelihood of an injunction would fall to 42 percent. Thus, procompetitive findings dramatically reduce the likelihood of a successful merger challenge. If the Herfindahl were closer to 2000 or if the court found another reason why collusion is unlikely, the probability an injunction would issue would fall even further. Moreover, if net competitive effect index was assigned to zero, a merger would have a 50 percent chance of being enjoined if the Herfindahl equaled 1709 when barriers to entry were present. This value approximates the 1800 level in the Guidelines, but the model clearly suggests that the courts look beyond Herfindahls to other structural conditions in all cases.[17]

Given a basic structure driving merger decisions, it is possible that underlying economic factors (barriers and competitive conditions) used in the court decisions are affected by various factors. For example, courts may be less willing to find barriers to entry under certain structural conditions. Likewise, courts may tend to make more findings associated with competitive conditions as economic analysis becomes more sophisticated over time. To explore the determinants of barriers and competitive conditions, econometric models of barriers to entry and competitive effects are estimated.

Analysis of Barriers to Entry

In a merger case, courts determine if barriers to entry are high by analyzing the structure of the market. This analysis can be simple, by searching for a single factor that forces the entrant to face higher costs than the incumbents or complex by evaluating sophisticated economic theories that suggest economies of scale interact with various other factors to render entry unprofitable (see DOJ and FTC Merger Guidelines (1992)). Buyer power is one important factor that can facilitate entry even in the presence of these sunk costs. The basic barrier model defines the likelihood of a barrier finding as a function of buyer power, conditions

---

[17] A simple analysis suggests that each condition compatible with an anticompetitive effect is equivalent to a 406 point increase in the Herfindahl. This result should be considered a lower bound for the impact of a condition compatible with competition. A much higher result of 711 points is obtained if the Herfindahl index is respecified to take the value zero for all Herfindahl cases under 2000. See footnote 16.

compatible or incompatible with collusion and the DOJ as a plaintiff (Kleit and Coate (1993)). Buyer power (BUY) is considered to be negatively related to barriers, because large buyers would be more likely to facilitate entry. The conditions related to collusion (COND) were defined as the total number of structural conditions addressed in the court case (the sum of the procompetitive and anticompetitive conditions). One could posit economically sophisticated judges would be more likely accept complicated barrier arguments so a positive sign is expected. Finally, the DOJ as a plaintiff variable would be expected to have a negative sign, given the DOJ's lower probability of showing barriers.[18]

The basic barrier model can also be expanded to determine how a preliminary injunction hearing (defined by a dummy variable which takes on the value one if the plaintiff files for a preliminary injunction and zero if the request is for a permanent injunction) affects the likelihood of a barrier finding. The preliminary injunction variable is expected to be positively related to a barrier finding, because courts may accept weaker evidence on barriers when only asked to issue a preliminary injunction against a transaction. This effect may also interact with the DOJ as a plaintiff, if the DOJ litigation problems are centered on the preliminary injunction cases. A negative sign would be expected for the interaction variable. The estimated equation is given

---

[18] Calkins (1988) addressed the DOJ litigation problems, but noted the problem had more to do with market definition.

below.

$$\text{BARRIERS} = \underset{(-1.56)}{-1.761} + \underset{(2.59)}{1.174} \text{ COND} + \underset{(.85)}{1.003} \text{ DOJ} - \underset{(-2.63)}{4.693} \text{ BUY} + \underset{(2.05)}{2.166} \text{ PI}$$

$$- \underset{(-2.17)}{4.93} \text{ DOJPI}$$

Pseudo R^2 = .5984   Chi-square = 29.24.

Most of the coefficients are clearly significant and the model easily passes the Chi-square test. The economic condition variable is positively linked to a barrier finding, while buyer power is strongly associated with easy entry. The preliminary injunction variable is positive, indicating that barrier findings are generally more likely in preliminary injunction cases. The DOJ's difficulty in showing barriers appears limited to preliminary injunction cases with the large negative coefficient outweighing both the insignificant DOJ coefficient and the positive impact associated with preliminary injunction cases. The model predicts a probability of a barrier finding below 50 percent for 9 of the 12 low barrier cases, while predicting a probability of over 50 percent for 27 of the 28 high barrier cases. Overall, the model predicts 90 percent of the cases correctly.

The basic regression equation closely matches Kleit and Coate (1993), suggesting that the model is robust to the addition of the private cases and the additional consideration given to preliminary injunction cases.[19] At the sample means for conditions, buyer

---

[19] Excluding the preliminary injunction variable generates a similar model given below (with t-statistics in parenthesis).
BARRIERS = .3250 (.70) + .7616 (2.31) COND - 3.196 (-2.61) BUY -
(continued...)

26

power and preliminary injunction status, the FTC or private parties project a 89 percent probability of a positive barrier finding, while the DOJ would show barriers in 19 percent of the cases. The number of conditions affects the likelihood of a barrier finding with a marginal finding above the mean raising the probability of a barrier finding to 99 percent for the FTC (or private parties) and to 62 percent for the DOJ and one marginal finding below the mean lowering the probability of a barrier finding to 44 percent and one percent respectively. The model also allows one to compute the marginal impact of buyer power. At the mean number of conditions and injunction status, the FTC or private parties maintain a 99 percent chance of success on the barrier issue if no finding of buyer power is made. However, if buyer power is present, the plaintiff would have only a one percent chance of showing barriers. The comparable results for the DOJ are 57 percent with no buyer power and less than one percent for buyer power. Thus, the finding of buyer power appears to have played a crucial role in merger analysis.

Litigation of a preliminary injunction has clear effects on the results, especially for the DOJ. In particular, the probability of a barrier finding falls from 80 percent to 3 percent holding the number of conditions and buyer power at their sample

---

[19](...continued)
1.289 (-2.08) DOJ (Pseudo R^2 = .4359, Chi- Square = 21.3). Using the means for the condition and buyer power variables, this model would suggest that the FTC and private or state plaintiffs have a 91 percent chance of showing barriers, while the DOJ would be successful 52 percent of the time.

means if the DOJ brings a preliminary injunction instead of a full merger challenge on the merits. Interestingly, in the late 1980s, the DOJ tended to move towards combined trials on the merits instead of preliminary injunctions in merger cases. For the FTC and private parties, the likelihood of a finding of high barriers increases from 44 percent to 98 percent if the average case is brought as a preliminary injunction instead of a full trial on the merits. Of course, even in a preliminary injunction, a barrier finding is unlikely if buyer power is present.

Analysis of Competitive Conditions

It is also possible to model conditions compatible or incompatible with anticompetitive effects from a merger. This would require two equations, because courts could make numerous findings supportive of either procompetitive or anticompetitive effects. As noted above, one dependent variable (For) is created by counting the number of findings compatible with an anticompetitive effect and the other dependent variable (Agst) is defined by identifying the number of findings compatible with competitive outcome. Both variables are modeled with the change in the Herfindahl, the DOJ as a plaintiff, a time index and the preliminary injunction status of the case. The change in the Herfindahl index (CHHI) is assumed to be negatively linked to the number of conditions related to either anticompetitive or competitive findings. In particular, as the change in the Herfindahl increases, detailed analyses of the competitive effects become marginally less useful and hence less likely to be incorporated into the court decision. The DOJ dummy variable is also included to test for differences across plaintiffs. The third variable, a time index defined as the number of months between the final merger decision and January 1982, allows for an increase in the number of factors both compatible and incompatible with collusion as courts obtain more familiarity with economic theory and the merger guidelines. A final variable proxies the effect of a preliminary injunction case on the opinion. One would expect preliminary injunction trials would have less detailed opinions, so the preliminary injunction variable should have a negative effect on both dependent variables.

Tobit models are estimated for the two equations.[20]

$$For = 1.225 - .0001586\ CHHI - 3.035\ DOJ + .01669\ Time - .9431\ PI$$
$$(1.13)(-.63)(-3.03)(1.2)(-1.16)$$

$$sigma = 2.024 \qquad Pseudo\ R^2 = .0772 \qquad Chi\text{-}square = 9.46$$

$$Agst = .6761 - .001074\ CHHI - .8195\ DOJ + .01518\ Time - 1.594\ PI$$
$$(.55)(-2.44)(-.88)(.99)(-1.86)$$

$$sigma = 2.122 \qquad Pseudo\ R^2 = .1239 \qquad Chi\text{-}square = 13.74.$$

Overall, the models generate few significant coefficients and explain roughly 10 percent of the variance in the dependent variables, however, both of the models have significant Chi-square

---

[20] The dependent variable in both equations is truncated at zero, so a tobit procedure is the appropriate estimation technique. The parameters of the model generate both a probability of a nonzero finding for the dependent variable and an expected value for the number of findings.

statistics. The models do generate a few interesting results. First, transactions that lead to large changes in the Herfindahl index do not appear to reduce significantly the number of findings suggestive of noncompetitive behavior (the For equation). On the other hand, the same variable tends to reduce the number of findings compatible with competition (the Agst equation). Thus, it appears that the court decisions are less likely to explain away the inference of noncompetitive behavior from the Herfindahl if the change is large. This result is not surprising, because considerations that protect a market from tacit collusion are not relevant for a dominant firm problem associated with a very high increase in the Herfindahl. Courts appear to accept significantly fewer findings compatible with noncompetitive behavior when the DOJ is the plaintiff. The total number of findings appears to increase with time, although the effects are not statistically significant. Finally, courts seem to make fewer findings compatible with competition in preliminary injunction hearings. Assigning the variables to their mean values, a preliminary injunction lowers the probability of a finding compatible with competition from 61 percent to 32 percent.

Much stronger results are obtained if one combines the number of conditions compatible with a noncompetitive effect with the number of conditions compatible with competition into the economic sophistication variable (COND). Retaining the change in the Herfindahl, the DOJ dummy variable, the time index and the preliminary injunction variable and adding an interaction variable

30

for the DOJ filing a preliminary injunction gives:

$$\begin{aligned}
\text{COND} = 3.179 &- .0005318\ \text{CHHI} - 3.187\ \text{DOJ} + .02826\ \text{Time} - 2.688\ \text{PI} \\
& (3.64) \quad (-2.39) \qquad\quad (-3.14) \qquad\quad (2.52) \qquad\quad (-3.38)
\end{aligned}$$

$$\begin{aligned}
&+ 3.0126\ \text{DOJPI} \\
&\quad (2.08)
\end{aligned}$$

$$\text{sigma} = 1.74 \qquad \text{Pseudo } R^2 = .1089 \qquad \text{Chi-square} = 17.98.$$

The variables are now all clearly significant, with the expected signs. The change in the Herfindahl variable tends to reduce the number of conditions cited by the court, suggesting that courts take a closer look at marginal cases. The DOJ variable exhibits a negative effect, implying that DOJ cases contain fewer economic findings. However, the DOJ effect disappears in the preliminary injunction cases, with all cases showing fewer economic findings. The time index is positively linked to the number of economic factors cited in court decision. Thus, the court's focus on economic issues appears to have increased, with the expected number of findings rising from two just after the June 1984 revision of the Guidelines to five after the April 1992 Guidelines revision for a full trial on the merits. On the other hand, the preliminary injunction cases contain fewer citations. In particular, only one finding related to competition was expected in a preliminary injunction case in June 1984 and this increased to three by April 1992.

V.   CONCLUSION

It appears that courts have focused on economic issues highlighted in the Merger Guidelines over the 1982-1992 period. The likelihood of a merger injunction increases with the Herfindahl

31

and decreases if barriers to entry are not present. The coefficients of the model suggest that the Herfindahl must approach 7000 (probably a single firm with a share of over 80 percent) for the plaintiff to have a chance of success without clear evidence on barriers to entry. This result clearly shows that entry evidence is very important. Moreover, the number of conditions related to competitive and noncompetitive behavior affects the outcome of the case. Merger challenges appear more likely to succeed if the established facts support collusion and less likely to succeed when the evidence shows collusion is difficult.

Econometric models also allow analysis of barriers to entry and competitive condition findings. The barrier model highlights the importance of buyer power in the entry barrier decision. However, it appears that lower standards are used to support a finding of barriers to entry in preliminary injunction cases. The competitive and collusive condition models suggest an increasing trend towards economic analysis as the sophistication of the courts grows with time. Fewer factors affecting competition seem to be cited in preliminary injunction cases. Thus, it appears that the preliminary injunction process disadvantages defendants, because the courts are less likely to find low barriers or conditions compatible with competition, either of which could lead to the dismissal of the case. On its face, this appears appropriate, because the preliminary injunction is just a temporary delay of a merger. In fact, the issuance of a preliminary injunction effectively forces the defendant to abandon the deal. Of the 15 successful preliminary injunctions, no transaction survived the full trial on the merits intact. Only PPG/Swedlow started an FTC administrative trial (but Swedlow was sold to a British firm during the trial, so the matter was withdrawn from litigation) and two private cases ended in settlements after the injunction was issued. Given that a preliminary injunction appears to enjoin a merger permanently, an argument can be made that courts should use the same standards in assessing preliminary injunctions as used in full trials on the merits.

A few other implications emerge from the analysis. First, the identity of the plaintiff appears to matter, with the DOJ exhibiting a lower success rate than others. This appears to be particularly true with respect to barriers to entry in preliminary injunction cases.

Second, identifying the party that appointed the judge does not seem to matter. The analysis shows the plaintiff's winning percentage is not related to the appointing party. More importantly, the underlying merits data do not appear to vary depending on which political party appointed the judge. This suggests that the quality of the cases does not appear to adjust to any anticipated political difference.

Finally, the evidence suggests that the standards for a merger injunction have not changed significantly over this period of time. The review of the data shows a similar winning percentage for plaintiffs both before and after 1987. Again, more detailed analysis of the underlying merits data suggest that the merits of the cases are statistically indistinguishable over the two time periods. Although the number of economic conditions linked to competitive effects appears to increase over time, these factors could be either pro or anticompetitive. Moreover, even though this index would suggest barrier findings were more likely, the trend would also increase the number of buyer power findings and reduce the likelihood of a barrier finding. Thus, the evidence does not support the hypothesis that merger injunctions are more difficult to obtain in the 1990s than in the 1980s.

BIBLIOGRAPHY

Bork, Robert, <u>The Antitrust Paradox: A Policy at War with Itself</u> (New York: Basic Books, 1978)

Blair, Roger D., David L. Kaserman, and Richard E. Romano, "A Pedagogical Treatment of Bilateral Monopoly," <u>Southern Economic Journal</u> 55(4) (April 1989) 831-841.

Calkins, Stephen, "Developments in Merger Litigation: The Government Doesn't Always Win," <u>Antitrust Law Journal</u> 56(3) Fall 1988 855-900.

Coate, Malcolm B., "Overview of the Merger Guidelines," <u>Journal of Reprints for Antitrust Law and Economics</u> 21(2) (1992). (A)

Coate, Malcolm B., "Economics, the Guidelines and the Evolution of Merger Policy," <u>Antitrust Bulletin</u>, 37(4) (Winter 1992) 997-1024 (B)

Coate, Malcolm B., and James A. Langenfeld, "Entry Under the Merger Guidelines, 1982-1992," <u>Antitrust Bulletin</u> 38(2) (Fall 1993).

Coate, Malcolm B., Andrew N. Kleit and Rene Bustamante "Fight, Fold or Settle?: Modeling the Reaction to FTC Merger Challenges," Federal Trade Commission Working Paper 200 (February 1993).

Cooter, Robert D. and Daniel L. Rubinfeld, "Economic Analysis of Legal Disputes and their Resolution," <u>Journal of Economic Literature</u> 27(3) (September 1989) 1067-1097.

Kleit, Andrew N. and Malcolm B. Coate, "Are Judges Leading Economic Theory: Sunk Costs, the Threat of Entry and the Competitive Process," <u>Southern Economic Journal</u> 60(1) (July 1993) 103-118.

Kovacic, William E., "Reagan's Judicial Appointments and Antitrust in the 1990's," <u>Fordham Law Review</u> 60(1) (October 1991) 49-124.

Langenfeld, James A. and Robert A. Rogowsky, "Settlement vs. Litigation in Antitrust Enforcement," in <u>Public Choice and Regulation: A View from Inside the Federal Trade Commission</u>, Robert Mackay, James Miller and Bruce Yandle, eds. (Hoover Institution Press: Stanford, Cal., 1987) 205-219.

Priest, George L. and Benjamin Klein "The Selection of Disputes for Litigation," <u>Journal of Legal Studies</u> 13(1) (January 1984) 1-55.

Steptoe, Mary Lou "The Power-Buyer Defense in Merger Cases," <u>Antitrust Law Journal</u> 61(2) (Winter 1993) 493-504.

Williamson, Oliver, "Efficiencies as an Antitrust Defense," <u>American Economic Review</u> 58(1) (March 1968) 18-36.

U.S. Department of Justice, "Department of Justice and Federal Trade Commission Horizontal Merger Guidelines," Antitrust Trade and Regulation Report, No. 1559, (April 2, 1992).

CASE CITATIONS

Brown Shoe v. U. S. 370 U. S. 294 (1962)

Consolidated Gold Fields v. Anglo American Corp., 698 F.Supp. 487 aff'd 1989-1 Trade Cas. (CCH) ¶ 68,500 (2nd Cir. 1989).

F.T.C. v. American Medical International et al., 104 F.T.C. 177 (1984).

F.T.C. v. R.R. Donnelley & Sons, Inc., 1990-1 Trade Cas. (CCH) ¶69,239 (D.D.C., August 27, 1990).

F.T.C. v. Echlin Manufacturing Co., 105 F.T.C. 410 (1985).

F.T.C. v. Elders Grain 691 F.Supp. 1131 aff'd 868 F.2d 901 (7th Cir. 1989).

F.T.C. v. Occidental Petroleum Corp., 1986-1 Trade Cas. (CCH) ¶ 67,071, (D.D.C., April 29, 1986).

F.T.C. v. Owens Illinois, 681 F.Supp. 27, (D.D.C. 1988)

F.T.C. v. PPG Industries, Inc., 628 F.Supp. 881, aff'd 798 F.2d 1500 (D.C.Cir 1986)

F.T.C. v. Promodes, 1989-2 Trade Cas. (CCH) ¶ 68,688 (N.D. Ga. Apr. 14, 1989)

F.T.C. v. University Health Inc, 1991-1 Trade Cas. (CCH) ¶69,444 rev'd 938 F.2d 1206 (11th Cir. 1991).

F.T.C. v. Weyerhaeuser, 1981-1 Trade Cas. (CCH) ¶ 63,974 aff'd 665 F.2d 1072 (D.C.Cir. 1981).

Monfort of Colorado v. Cargill 591 F. Supp. 683 (1983) aff'd, 761 F. 2d 570 (1985) rev'd 479 U.S. 104 (1986).

R. C. Bigelow v. Unilever N.V., 689 F.Supp. 76, aff'd, 867 F.2d 102 (2d Cir. 1989), cert. denied, 493 U.S. 815 (1989).

U. S. v. Archer-Daniels-Midland Co., 695 F.Supp. 1000 (S.D. Iowa 1987), rev'd, 866 F.2d 242 (8th Cir. 1988), cert denied 493 U. S. 809 (1990), remanded 781 F. Supp. 1400 (S. D. Iowa 1991).

U. S. v. Baker Hughes, 731 F.Supp. 3, aff'd, 908 F.2d 981 (D.C.Cir. 1990).

U. S. v. Calmar, 612 F.Supp. 1298 (D.C. NJ 1985).

U. S. v. Carilion Health System, 707 F.Supp. 840 (W.D. Vir. 1989)

U. S. v. Country Lake Foods, 1990-2 Trade Cas. (CCH) ¶ 69,113 (D.Minn. June 1, 1990).

U. S. v. General Dynamics Corp., 415 U.S. 486 (1974).

U. S. v. Philadelphia National Bank, 374 U.S. 321 (1963).

U. S. v. Syufy Enterprises, 712 F.Supp. 1386, *aff'd*, 903 F.2d 659 (9th Cir. 1990).

U. S. v. Waste Management, 588 F.Supp. 498 *rev'd* 743 F.2d 976 (2d Cir. 1984).

U. S. v. Von's Grocery, 384 U. S. 270 (1966).

Table 1 Overview of Merger Challenges

	DOJ	FTC	Private	Total
Cases	15	20(14)	13	48
% Won	27%[1,2]	65% (71%)	62%	52%
% Won, Preliminary Injunction	20%[1,2]	71% (71%)	67%	73%
% Won Full Trial on Merits	30%	50%(-)	0%	35%
% Won, Court Republican	38%	64% (75%)	71%	59%
% Won, Court Democratic	14%[1]	67% (67%)	50%	42%
% Won before 1/1/1987	20%	67% (80%)	57%	52%
% Won after 1/1/1987	30%	64% (67%)	67%	52%
% Markets Established	67%	90% (86%)	62%	75%
% Won given market	40%[2]	72% (83%)	100%	69%

1 The mean of the DOJ variable is significantly different from the mean of the FTC variable.
2 The mean of the DOJ variable is significantly different from the mean of the private variable.
3 The mean of the FTC variable is significantly different from the mean of the private variable.

Table 2 Analysis of Economic Findings

	DOJ	FTC	Private	Total
Cases	12	19 (13)	9	40
% Won	33%[1,2]	68% (77%)	89%	63%
Herfindahl (HHI)	3936	3688 (4103)	3948	3821
Change in HHI	1321	1291 (1496)	1341	1311
% with Barriers	42%[1]	84% (85%)	78%	70%
% with Efficiencies	42%	26% (38%)	11%	28%
% with Buyer Power	33%	21% (23%)	11%	23%
Conditions Anticompetitive (For)	.58[1]	1.84 (1.31)	1.22	1.33
Conditions Procompetitive (Against)	1.33[2]	1.00 (.62)	.33	.95
Net Conditions	-1.16[1,2]	.58 (.31)	.78	.10

1 The mean of the DOJ variable is significantly different from the mean of the FTC variable.
2 The mean of the DOJ variable is significantly different from the mean of the private variable.
3 The mean of the FTC variable is significantly different from the mean of the private variable.
2

www.ingramcontent.com/pod-product-compliance
Lightning Source LLC
Chambersburg PA
CBHW081312180526
45170CB00007B/2672